AF303903

How Social Media Almost Destroyed My Relationship — and Why It Could Happen to You, Too

Gwendoline P Point

How Social Media Almost Destroyed My Relationship — and Why It Could Happen to You, Too

<u>Trigger Warning:</u>

This guide covers topics that may be emotionally challenging for some readers, including issues of trust, emotional hurt, and the impact of social media on relationships. If you feel uncomfortable with these topics, please take your time reading and take breaks as needed.

Introduction:

A few weeks ago, our relationship faced a serious crisis. A woman repeatedly messaged my husband on TikTok, eventually going so far as to send him an intimate video. This unexpected and painful experience deeply affected both of us and put our partnership to a serious test—so much so that our relationship almost didn't survive it. In this guide, I want to help you better understand and manage the impact of social media on relationships. We will discuss sensitive topics such as intimate content, unwanted messages, and the emotional challenges they can bring with them.

The Moment That Changed Everything

I'll never forget that Wednesday evening, June 5, 2024. For days, I had sensed that something in our relationship had shifted, but I couldn't pinpoint exactly what. I sat down on the gray couch outside our bedroom, and only then did I notice Roli's shorts lying there.

That's when I spotted his phone, and from that moment on, nothing was the same. Long story short: I had just found confirmation of my suspicions. Dozens of love messages from a woman I'd never heard of. She'd even sent a video. I knew exactly what I was about to see, but I couldn't stop myself from opening it. I knew I was about to hurt myself, yet I watched. Like a lightning bolt, the video struck me full force. In seconds, a wave of sadness washed over me, mixed with anger, confusion, and fear. My body felt hot and cold at the same time. I was sweating and shivering as tears filled my eyes and my legs shook in sync with my pounding heart. Roli, who was in the shower, yanked the curtain open as I stormed into the bathroom. He looked at me with wide, questioning eyes. Without letting him speak or step out, I shoved his phone in his face and demanded, "What is this?" He glanced at the screen, clearly overwhelmed, and shrugged his shoulders. In that moment, a thousand thoughts flashed through my mind, and I acted on one of them immediately: I tapped the screen to call her.

After a single ring, an older woman's voice answered cheerfully, "Yes, hello?" My stomach clenched instantly. It was the voice of the woman who, only moments before, had been rubbing herself all over her body on that video. Fury consumed me, and without thinking, I heard myself say, "Hello, this is Roli's wife. Do you know he's married?"

Silence hung on the other end for a moment, and then I heard her reply, "Yes," followed by a laugh—a laugh that sounded to me like an ugly hyena's cackle. Then she hung up.

Fuming, I hit redial, and once again, that infuriating voice answered. As soon as her voice reached my ears, I yelled, "What kind of videos are you sending my husband, you…!" What followed was a string of curses and white-hot rage pouring out of me. After a few seconds, she hung up again without another word. I had no patience to continue with her, so I let it go, turning my attention to my husband instead. He stood there, dripping and wrapped in a towel, unable to meet my gaze.

I stormed up the stairs to the bedroom and waited for him to follow. With each passing second, my disappointment grew—disappointment in how I had completely misjudged him. Nervously, I sat on the bed, looking at Roli, who met my gaze with a pained expression. Despite my anger, I tried to keep my composure to talk things through with him. It was late, though, and the kids were asleep downstairs, so I had to hold myself back, as hard as it was. Still, we talked— or rather, I snapped at him while he tried to defend himself. After nearly an hour, we both realized that continuing the conversation wouldn't help, so we decided to pick it up the next day. The thought of leaving things unresolved weighed heavily on my heart. I felt as if we were talking in circles without reaching any real solution. In the hours that followed, I reflected on Roli and what he truly meant to me.

To Better Understand Roli: A Few Words About the Man by My Side

Roli is a fantastic listener, a true problem solver, a loving father, and my personal dream man. He has a strong desire to help others, often making hasty decisions—which only makes him more human in my eyes. This mix of helpfulness and spontaneity allows him to form new connections incredibly quickly. Women see in him the empathetic man they have always sought, and for many men, he becomes the friend they can count on.

Usually, all of this isn't a problem for me; I love his openness. However, difficulties arise when he fails to set clear boundaries, especially in situations that could spiral into a disaster, like the current one. He sometimes leaves it too open for too long that he isn't looking for something new, and he reacts too late when others' feelings get out of control. This hurts me, even though I know it's not his intention.

In our modern world, where many people lose themselves in social media and communicate less with each other, it's understandable that women are attracted to him. He gives them the attention they crave. However, that in no way justifies what has happened—neither from their side nor from his. The video was a clear breach of trust, and it will take me a lot of time, strength, and tears to process it all. But I know deep down that he didn't mean any harm.

What It Feels Like When the World Around You Crumbles

I can tell you how it feels. For me, it played out like this: The night stretches on endlessly, and sleep eludes me. Even though I lie in bed, I can't shake off the thoughts. The images from the video keep replaying in my mind over and over. I toss and turn, unable to find peace, and the sadness that hangs over me is suffocating. Roli sleeps on the other side of the bed, and as I look at him, tears fill my eyes. How could he do this to me? What could have driven him to communicate with another woman, let alone share such intimate things with her? The questions torment me. I feel trapped in this nightmare with no way out.

As dawn breaks, I get up to avoid falling apart on the spot. The kids are still asleep, giving me a moment of silence. I prepare breakfast, but every bite seems to get stuck in my throat. My thoughts are a chaotic mess, and I can't focus on anything.

When the kids finally come into the living room, I try to organize my thoughts. I smile as best as I can and do my best to keep up appearances. Yet inside me, a storm is raging. While I play and laugh with the children, I feel lonelier than ever. This inner turmoil becomes my undoing. I fight back tears as I read them stories.

Roli is in the background, lost in his own thoughts. He has apologized, and his remorse seems genuine, but I can't forgive him. The distance between us is palpable, and the more I think about it, the more I know that nothing will ever be the same again.

What Lessons Have I Learned?

It's important to prioritize yourself and your feelings. You need to understand that it's okay to be vulnerable and to take time for yourself to heal from these wounds.

What Can You Do in This Situation?

Seek a conversation with your partner to share your emotions and create a space for understanding. It may be difficult, but open communication can help clear up misunderstandings and find ways to move forward together.

I called in sick to work because I wouldn't be able to accomplish anything productive anyway. Luckily, I have an understanding employer, so at least that's not a problem. Now, Roli and I sit across from each other on the couch, discussing everything once again. I try to convey my perspective while he attempts to explain how it all got to this point. In this moment, it's incredibly hard for me to believe that he didn't intend to hurt me or that he wanted to end our relationship. But when I think about all the secret messages and phone calls, what he says just doesn't match up with what he's done.

Though it hurts my heart, I think in that moment that I probably will never be able to trust him again. The hours pass, and we go around in circles. So, we decide to take a break and focus on something else. He goes to the workshop without his phone, and I try to process my thoughts through writing. It's to no avail. This entire situation has triggered a massive writer's block within me. I keep seeing the video in my mind, that ugly creature writhing and moaning. My mental imagery resembles a horror film from which I cannot escape. I see the door, but I just can't reach it.

Frustrated and angry, I slam my laptop shut so hard that the loud bang startles me. For a moment, I hold my breath—did I just break the screen? That's exactly what I need right now! A quick glance at the monitor, however, reveals that everything is fine.

But inside me, nothing is fine. I feel my thoughts tightening around the same topic until I can't form a coherent thought anymore. My writer's block begins to creep in—slowly at

first, then overwhelmingly. What I don't know in that
moment is that this block will accompany me for weeks.
Again and again, I sit down, hoping to escape into other
thoughts - but it never works. The video, the messages, her
voice - everything repeats endlessly in my mind as if it's
stalking me. Every attempt to rid myself of these images
fails. I spiral into frustration and helplessness. It feels like
I'm sliding uncontrollably into depression.
Everyday life with Roli is becoming increasingly
burdensome. We argue more frequently, and my jealousy
develops into a dimension that feels foreign to me—a ugly,
destructive side of myself that I can barely control. Each
time his phone lights up, a wave of mistrust and anger
washes over me. I can't help but explode, questioning who is
reaching out to him. My trust is shattered, while my jealousy
reaches unmanageable heights. Even small things set me off:
if I call him and he doesn't answer immediately, I lose
control.

My thoughts race, and I imagine the worst. This can't
continue - this situation is consuming me and threatens to
destroy everything that connects us. That woman has
awakened an ugly side in me that I can barely keep at bay.
No matter how hard I try to push her out of my mind, she
remains ever-present. Whether I'm alone or talking with
Roli, she's there, always lurking like a shadow in the
background. It feels as if she hovers around us like a thick,
suffocating cloud, continuously accompanying us and
refusing to disappear.

Still, I try not to let this filth get the better of me. Although
the video borders on emotional abuse, I don't want my

thoughts to distract me further from him. But I've learned that there are ways to cope with these painful feelings and to rebuild our trust in each other.

Here are some practical tips that have helped us cope with jealousy and strengthen our relationship:

1. **Open Communication:**

   Talk to your partner about your feelings instead of keeping them bottled up. Honesty fosters trust and understanding.

2. **Setting Boundaries:**

   Define what types of interactions with others are acceptable and which are not. Clear boundaries help avoid misunderstandings.

3. **Self-Reflection:**

   Take time to understand your own feelings and insecurities. Engaging with yourself can help prevent emotional outbursts.

Friday, June 7

Today, I have to go back to work, whether I like it or not. I can't afford to stay home too long. Physically, I'm present in the office, but mentally? Forget it. It's impossible for me to accomplish anything today. My phone lies beside me on the desk, practically screaming for me to message Roli. Every attempt to ignore it fails miserably.

Like an addict waiting for the next "hit," I keep reaching for the phone and staring at the black screen. Eventually, I can no longer resist the urge and send Roli a message. But I don't write like a rational woman; no, I write like a typical woman filled with rage, wanting to make it clear to my husband just how unhappy I am with the entire situation. Naturally, I'm convinced: "If I phrase it this way, he will finally understand!"

In my frustration, I type so quickly that my message is riddled with typos, as if a child wrote it. And his response? Calm and matter-of-fact: "Honey, let's talk about this later. You need to focus on your work. I love you."
"You love me? Seriously? Is he mocking me?" Of course, I can't let that slide. Not only do I send him one angry message after another, but I also vent my frustrations on TikTok. Every hateful thought I have about that "hyena" is written down, accompanied by an image, and uploaded to TikTok. Naturally, I tag her in the post.

I don't hold out much hope that my post will go viral, as my views usually range between 200 and 800. But then, during my break, I discover an incredible fact: my video has over

800 views in just two and a half hours, 74 likes, and what surprises me the most, 18 comments! Less than an hour later, the views surpass 2000, and the likes and comments are soaring. I've never experienced anything like it.

Dumbfounded, I begin reading and responding to every single comment during my break. The feedback is overwhelming and reinforces my belief that I did something right - though it may not have been the best way to handle my feelings. The first comment shows me just how much it resonates with people: "You're speaking my mind. I feel for you. I've been through the same thing. Wishing you strength."

This post will not be the last, as I continue to publish content in the following days, venting my frustrations, feelings, or bad mood on TikTok. The comments vary from positive to merely being a smiley face, but that doesn't bother me at all.

What particularly pleases me - though I know it's not exactly noble - is that the hyena sees every single one of my posts. Time and again, we receive messages from various sources that she is not happy about how I'm discussing this situation. Her reaction motivates me to keep going. My desire for revenge has been awakened. I want to pay her back just as she has hurt me.

Roli, who is slowly starting to have a problem with my way of handling this, increasingly warns me that I should address this differently than on TikTok. What does he think he's

doing? They both chose to act like jerks, and now I'm
supposed to keep it together? Yeah, right!
I have a strong tendency toward vindictiveness. If you lay
your hands on what's important to me or take something
precious from me, then I hope our paths don't cross.
Because if they do, you will feel the consequences. I know
my behavior is far from right, but my character isn't exactly
uncomplicated.

In the meantime, I know that this path of revenge helps no
one - least of all myself. But once the pain and anger are
ignited, it's hard for me to regain control. It feels as if a wall
has been built around my heart to protect me from further
pain, but it also keeps all the good feelings outside. Yet this
cycle of anger and revenge comes at a cost.

I realize how much I am hardening internally and losing
touch with the people who are important to me.
Roli, in particular, suffers from my behavior. He wants to
help; he wants to support me, but I keep pushing him away.
Somehow, it seems my pride, or perhaps my pain, is greater
than the desire for reconciliation. But how did it come to
this? I wasn't always like this. I used to not take every little
thing to heart. But after all the disappointments and hurts,
something inside me has turned cold. It's as if I have crossed
a line from which there is no turning back.

And yet I ask myself, "Why should I be the one to change?
Why do the people who get hurt always have to bear the
responsibility for healing? They started it. They put me in
this position, and now I'm just supposed to overlook it?

An important lesson that I unfortunately learned too late is…

that revenge does not bring true liberation. As tempting as it may be to throw pain back at others, in the end, it only poisons oneself.

Vera F. Birkenbihl once said:

"If I'm upset about something for more than 15 seconds, then I am responsible for it myself. Because from that moment on, I decide whether to let go of the anger or carry it with me."

And that is precisely true. It is up to us whether we hold on to anger or let it go in order to find peace again.

Five days of hell on earth have passed, but the situation has hardly improved. I lie in bed crying when Roli comes in to comfort me. For us, a brief but significant conversation takes place. His eyes reveal that he is not doing well either and that this whole situation has also thrown him off balance.

I want to save this relationship. I love him and don't want to lose or give up on him. I know he loves me and that he certainly didn't intend to hurt me with his actions—that much I understand. If only I could explain or show him how I feel inside! Yet at the same time, I cannot see into him. However, his eyes betray him, and I can clearly see how he is feeling.

Every time I look at him, that feeling comes alive again - the same feeling I had more than 15 years ago when our eyes first met. My heart instantly races, and my features soften, just like my knees do when I think of him.

But despite all this love, here I stand, in the middle of a storm I never could have imagined. I keep asking myself: How could it come to this? Why did we allow outside influences - people who have nothing to do with us - to intrude so deeply into our relationship? And yet I know that it's not just about those other people. It's about us. About our trust, our communication, our boundaries.

What hurts me the most is the uncertainty. That nagging feeling that I don't know if I can ever fully trust him again.

Not because I think he wants to cheat on me, but because
he struggles to truly understand my feelings. I see it in his
eyes—he regrets what happened, but he doesn't understand
why it affects me so deeply. Perhaps it's because he hasn't
yet realized how much he loses himself in those social
networks. A fleeting glance, an innocent comment, and yet
it's enough to hurt me.

Then there's this inner struggle - one voice telling me to stay
strong and give him a chance, while another warns me
against opening up again, only to possibly be disappointed
once more. How can I approach him when I also fear being
hurt?

I know we can get through this. I know we can make it if we
are both willing to work on it. But for that, we have to be
honest, especially with ourselves. Perhaps that is the hardest
step. To recognize that we are not perfect, that we have
made mistakes, and that it's not enough to simply move on
as if nothing has happened.
It takes time, patience, and the willingness to truly engage
with one another - without walls, without secrets.

Do you know that feeling of not being understood?

It's frustrating, isn't it? If you've experienced this too, then
the following might help:
Talk openly with your partner, even if it's difficult.
Sometimes, it's easier for us to suffer in silence or hide our
feelings out of fear of appearing weak or vulnerable. But
only by being honest and sharing your feelings can your
partner truly understand what you're going through. It's
important to explain to your partner why their behavior

hurts you and how it affects you. At the same time, try to understand their perspective - often it's not malice but ignorance or a lack of sensitivity that causes us pain. Another key element is trust - it cannot be rebuilt overnight, but it can be developed slowly and patiently. Try to take small steps toward openness and intimacy. And when doubts or fears arise, express them immediately instead of burying them inside.

Make sure to take conscious time for yourself to sort out your thoughts. It's easy to lose your clarity in an emotional whirlwind. But when you find a moment of calm, you'll often realize that the solution lies not only in working on the relationship but also in how you respond to conflicts.

In short!
Talk to each other, listen to one another, and work on rebuilding trust step by step. Injuries don't heal on their own—they require time and effort. But if both partners are willing to walk this path together, they can overcome any crisis.

<u>**Monday, June 17.**</u>
When almost everything descends into chaos

The repercussions of the incident are showing up not just in my personal life, but also at work. I work in shipping and accounting, where I am responsible for processing orders that come in online, over the phone, or by mail. Since our team is quite small, a lot of the responsibility falls on me. Normally, I have a good overview, but since the incident, more and more mistakes are creeping into my work. The worst part is that these errors often only become apparent days or weeks later, when customers reach out or orders go awry. The stress in my head affects my concentration so much that it becomes difficult to keep track of everything. Especially on Mondays and Tuesdays, the most stressful days of the week, it's almost impossible to handle the flood of tasks without making mistakes.

There are weeks when I incorrectly process a series of orders, and then there are phases when everything runs relatively smoothly. But the fear that something will go wrong constantly lingers over me.

Additionally, in the days following the incident, I was constantly distracted by private messages with Roli. Although I knew I should focus on work, I simply couldn't. My thoughts kept spiraling around what had happened. I replayed the video in my mind over and over, and the ugly grin of that woman echoed in my ears.

Each new conversation with Roli pulled me out of my workflow, preoccupying me so much that it was impossible to fully disengage from work.

This Can Help Calm the Situation

Leave Your Phone in Your Jacket

Bag, or Better Yet, in the Car! This way, you can avoid distractions. When you talk to your partner or spend time together, focus entirely on the moment. By putting your phone out of sight, you minimize distractions and create an atmosphere of trust and closeness that is essential for a healthy relationship.

When Jealousy Takes Over

It Can Help to Pause and View the Situation Objectively. Ask yourself: Is my jealousy based on facts or just on assumptions and fears? Sometimes, it helps to mentally distance yourself before reacting.

I know it sounds simple to say, "Stay calm," "Take a deep breath," and all those well-meaning pieces of advice - blah, blah, blah... But honestly, I've found that all of this doesn't help when you're boiling with anger, disappointed, or furiously sending messages. It usually just makes the situation worse.

I also have to admit that I have a particular talent for getting really caught up in things. And as if that weren't enough, I manage to provoke the other person so that they switch off and don't listen to me properly or read my messages completely - or at least not understand them correctly. But fortunately, there's the genius who invented voice messaging. It makes arguing much better! Every emotion comes across much more clearly than when you're typing. But joking aside, it's really wise to calm down first before writing anything. Or even better, don't write at all and discuss the issue in person when you're face to face.

<u>**Practical Example, how Emotions Affect Work:**</u>

I usually enjoy going to work because I love my job, my colleagues, and the customers - just everything. It suits me perfectly. But today is one of those days that has been doomed to fail since I woke up. Yesterday was also a terrible day. I had yet another argument with Roli, and not in an erotic, beautiful way - no, we really fought.

As a result, I didn't sleep well and cursed the alarm clock this morning. When I arrive at the office, I have no idea what catastrophe is brewing. However, not even two hours later, I'm in the office and receive my first reprimand. Me and a reprimand? Something like that has never happened to me! Completely taken aback, I sit there, almost stammering and fighting back tears with all my might, trying not to break down like a wilting flower. I pull myself together as best as I can and try to get through the rest of the day without making any mistakes.

But you know the feeling: the harder you try to do everything right, the more mistakes happen. That's exactly how the entire Monday unfolds. When I finally finish work, I realize on the way home that I forgot the toast bread that Roli specifically asked me to bring this morning. He reminded me of it again, but it still remains on the shelf in the store as I come home without any bread.

As soon as I step through the door, Roli immediately notices that I must have had a bad day - perhaps from the way I'm cursing in the hallway after dropping my car keys and then my phone. Or maybe he has developed a sixth sense for recognizing when I'm in a bad mood - who knows?

In any case, he immediately heads to the store to give me a little space to breathe. These are the moments when I realize how much we love each other. Roli could have easily lost his composure, blamed me, or made a scene over the forgotten bread - after all, he had reminded me about it this morning. But that's just Roli. Instead of complaining, he simply goes out and takes care of it.

And that's not all: he not only brings back the bread but also fills up my car, gets me a soda, and brings something for the kids to drink. Without saying a word about it, he sets everything on the table. Then he comes into the kitchen, grabs a wooden spoon, and helps me with cooking. But before he starts preparing, he pulls me into his arms and quietly asks, "Do you want to tell me what happened at work today?"

His gaze is so loving and understanding that I almost burst into tears. Instead of speaking, I just shrug and stare at the floor. "Oh, sweetheart," he whispers, "everything will be alright." With a big kiss, he seals this moment of care.
In this moment, I feel as if the weight of the day is falling from my shoulders. His affection and support give me the strength to leave the day behind me. I know I can rely on him, no matter how challenging the situation is. These small gestures of love and care are what strengthen our relationship and bring us closer together.

Regular conversations about daily life and one's own feelings are important to avoid misunderstandings and strengthen the emotional connection.

Take time for each other to talk about the highs and lows of the day. These conversations foster understanding and intimacy between partners.

<u>Tuesday, June 18th</u>

In recent days, we have grown closer several times. We've talked a lot, and slowly we are starting to find solid ground under our feet again. Each conversation brings us a little closer together, and I feel the walls that have formed between us slowly crumbling. It feels like we are not only discussing our fears and worries but also the love that connects us. We make time to simply be together, without pressure and without the shadow of the past days. Even though our laughter is sometimes a bit strained, I can feel my heart slowly blooming for him again.

However, despite these advances, there are still moments when I pause. A remnant of uncertainty gnaws at me, which doesn't just want to go away. It's not that I don't trust him, but the wound that has formed takes longer to heal than I had hoped.

Every time his phone vibrates or he receives a message, a quiet doubt sneaks into my thoughts. I try to push it aside because I want to save this relationship, but it's hard to let go completely.

Tonight, while we are sitting on the couch watching a movie, I feel the urge to steer the conversation back to what has been weighing us down. I don't want to, but it's as if I need one last confirmation. Maybe I need that to finally find peace. Perhaps I want to ask him, "Have you really moved on? Is there anything I should know?" But I swallow the words. It feels wrong to ruin this moment when things are starting to get better again. Nevertheless, that thought lingers, like a knot in my stomach.

Suddenly, he notices that I am tense. His eyes fix on me, and I feel his unspoken question hanging in the air. "What's wrong? You seem so restless," he asks quietly. It's as if he can see the shadow in my thoughts that hangs over us. "Nothing," I say reflexively, but his penetrating gaze shows me that he doesn't believe that. Finally, I sigh and give in, opening the door to all the thoughts that have burdened us for so long. "I'm just worried…" I begin, and immediately I feel his attention intensifying as if he has been waiting for this moment.

Again, we talk about everything that has happened - the same issues that won't let us go. The longer I talk about it, the more everything inside me tightens. Why do I feel trapped in this endless cycle? Time and again, I am the one who reopens the wounds that won't heal.

"I'm sorry that I have to bring this up again," I finally say, my voice trembling. "But I just can't find peace. It's eating me up."
His face softens, and he pulls me into a loving embrace. "I understand," he murmurs, and I feel that he truly means it. He tries to understand me, yet at the same time, I know I don't want to burden him further with my doubts.

Slowly, I begin to realize that constantly rehashing the past won't get us anywhere. The path to healing might not lie in always talking about what has happened, but in accepting that we are both still in the healing process. With a deep breath, I lean against him, trying to release some of my inner pressure. Yet the thought that I can't keep having these conversations remains like a quiet shadow in the back of my mind that isn't easily dispelled.

There are moments in a relationship when you feel trapped, as if you are running in the same circle. You feel like the conversations are repeating themselves, and the pressure to clarify things keeps growing.

Even if it feels awful and you don't want to start all over again, there is an inner urge that you should follow. Don't ignore the signals your gut is sending you.
It's okay to seek clarity, even if it's uncomfortable. Sometimes love requires us to address the same issues repeatedly to clear up misunderstandings and alleviate fears. But be aware that it is also important to find a healthy balance. If you notice that you are going in circles and getting nowhere, it can also be helpful to take a break.

<u>Ask yourself:</u>

What does this conversation really bring me? Do I feel better after the exchange, or do I just feel exhausted? If you feel that the constant discussions are no longer helping, then it's time to choose a different approach.
Sometimes it's better to give yourself and your partner the space to grow and heal, rather than constantly reopening the wounds.

No matter how many times you fall, what matters is that you

get up and keep going. Ultimately, you are the one who must decide what is best for you and your relationship. Listen to your heart and let it guide you.

<u>**A few days later**</u>

I sit down at my laptop again, trying to write down my thoughts and experiences from the past few weeks. It's harder than I thought. The words swirl around in my head, but I just can't get a clear, coherent sentence on paper. With each failed attempt, my frustration pounds harder on the keyboard. This can't be true! I, who writes so often, should at least be able to put together a decent sentence that makes sense.

Completely absorbed in my own world, I notice too late that Roli has sat down next to me and is looking at me with a questioning expression. I abruptly stop typing as he holds out his phone to me and says, "Please take a look at this." Immediately, an uneasy feeling spreads inside me.

Oh no, what has she done this time?

This miserable person has been posting videos for days, where she depressingly shows her face to the camera and sings love songs.

Ugh, what a scary person!

Of course, I immediately think of her. Who else could it be? But Roli has something else to show.
Hesitantly, I take the phone and press play. It's a duet video featuring the woman who has fallen for Roli. She is singing with another person, and the video has an unmistakable title:

"WE ARE NOT FRIENDS! YOU FAKE SNAKE, HITTING ON MARRIED MEN!"

Further down it says:

"Anyone who attacks my friends will have to deal with me."

She tagged Roli and even me. I look at Roli in astonishment, who is looking at me with a satisfied smile.
"Who is that?" I ask, surprised.
"That's someone from my group," he replies calmly.
I stare at him with my mouth agape.
"But... I don't even know her! How can she know about this?" My head is a complete mess.
"Have you talked to her?" I finally ask.
"No," he answers casually, shaking his head.
It takes me a long moment to piece everything together.
"But how can she know?"

"Well," he begins to explain, "your posts, as well as the conversations with the other admins in the group, quickly made the rounds. Many members noticed that something had happened. Some asked questions that we answered as neutrally as possible. After all, we didn't want to make it widely known that she has a crush on me and sent this video. For privacy reasons and to protect her."

As he utters the word **"protection,"** I feel my anger flare up again. Protection? The word echoes in my head, triggering a flood of emotions. And what about me? Where was my protection?

Inside, I am boiling. No one helped me, no one warned me! The thought strikes me. It feels as if I have been completely left alone while everyone else knew and simply remained silent.

I am about to say something when he adds, "I wanted you to see this so you realize that you're not alone."
I glance back at the phone and read the words once more. A mix of anger, sadness, and relief washes over me.
It deeply moves me that someone is finally standing up for me. But even more surprising is that this woman, who doesn't even know me personally, is making such a clear statement. Her words hit the mark.

But what might surprise me the most is the fact that this won't be the last video of this kind that she posts. She'll continue to take a stand, showing her full support for me— even though we've never met.
And as if that weren't enough, she'll eventually join my TikTok group, "Wortmagnet," and become an active admin there.

But I'll tell you more about that later. For now, I just need to process everything that has happened.

<u>**Saturday, June 22nd**</u>

Lost in thought, I'm tidying up the kitchen when Roli quietly comes over and just stands there, looking at me. It takes me a moment to realize he's by my side, watching me with a loving smile. His gaze, so innocent and clear, draws me in, and I take a step closer to him. Instantly, he pulls me in and kisses me with fervor.

He wraps his arms around my waist, and his scent fills my senses. He smells incredible - almost too good - and in that moment, I let go of the pain, frustration, and disappointment, allowing myself to be swept away by a sense of lightness. Slowly, he begins kissing my neck, working his way softly up to my chin.

My breathing quickens as his hands hold me tighter. For a brief moment, I almost forget everything that's happened between us in the past days - but only almost, as suddenly that disgusting voice echoes in my mind again, and I see those images flashing before my eyes. Disgusted, I squeeze my eyes shut and shudder a bit.

Roli interprets my reaction as encouragement and goes a step further. And that's fine for the moment, as his actions - how he swiftly lifts me onto the kitchen counter and kisses me passionately - pull me right back into the present. Then, things happen quickly. Clothes are tossed aside, one kiss follows another, and before I know it, we find ourselves on the sofa. Entwined, breathless, we lie wrapped in each other's arms.

Suddenly, it's just us again. Not the arguing couple that was caught up in a heated fight only a few hours earlier. No, we're back to being the two people who love each other deeply and face every challenge together. I'm still in his arms, held so tightly that getting up seems impossible.
I smile up at him, and he looks back at me with a satisfied glow. As he gently strokes my arm, I hear his soft voice say, "I am so, so sorry, my love. I hope you believe me when I say I never wanted to hurt you." Without looking away from me, he takes a deep breath and wipes away a tear that quickly trails down his cheek. "I'll never let you go. You're the best decision of my life, and I love you. You're my little mangorindli."

When I hear this old nickname, which he gave me so many years ago, I feel a tingling in my stomach that spreads warmly through my entire body. It's the same feeling I had when he first kissed me. Back then, I was leaning against his car as he braced his hands on either side of me, coming closer and closer until his lips gently touched mine. That exact same feeling washes over me now, and suddenly, my thoughts transport me right back to that time - to the place where we first kissed.

Wondering how I got this nickname?

Only someone a bit out of their mind could come up with something like that - lovingly meant, of course.
I remember the situation exactly: I was wearing a black tank top, and we were standing in the hallway after a long, exhausting day of moving. He took me in his arms to thank

me for all the work and rested his head on my shoulder. Instantly, he said, "Mmm, you smell so good."
He quickly sniffed along my neck, from my collarbone to the other side, inhaling deeply, and as he exhaled, I could feel his warm breath spreading across my neck. It was as if this scent had stirred something in him, because he suddenly wrapped his arms around me with such intensity that I nearly lost my balance and had to steady myself against the wall.

But Roli was holding me so firmly that falling over wasn't really an option. At most, we'd topple over together—but luckily, that didn't happen. He murmured again, "You smell like… like a tangerine and… a mango." Meanwhile, I thought I must smell like anything but an exotic fruit.
After all the lifting, carrying, and driving back and forth, I felt I was sweating more than a construction worker under the blazing sun. How on earth could I smell good? But what do I know?

The only thing I was sure of was how utterly wiped out I felt after hauling things around all day. Sweating more than usual, I felt the opposite of "sniffable." But apparently, he saw things differently.

He leaned in to sniff me once more, almost like a man possessed, and then said, "Now I know - you are…" he took another deep breath, "You're my little Mangorindli" Positively surprised, I smiled at him and asked for confirmation: "I'm what?" He lifted his head, looked at me with complete adoration, and replied, "My little Mangorindli"

And from that day on, I was his "Mangorindli."
That day, he reminded me that no matter how exhausting or lousy a day might be, there's always a reason to laugh, to joke, and to let go of the daily grind together.
By the way, this name is actually engraved inside his wedding ring:

"Mangorindli 08/24/12"

Smile and Laugh Together

Humor can be a powerful remedy against jealousy. Try to bring lightness back into your relationship by regularly planning activities that make you laugh together. Every smile, every tender glance, gives me hope that we can find our way out of this dark phase together.

The feeling of being a team grows stronger, and I begin to believe in us - in the strength of our relationship. These conversations are like small glimmers of light in the darkness, reminding us why we first fell in love. And although the shadows of the past haven't completely faded, I feel that together, we can work to dispel them. As long as we communicate openly and honestly, there's hope that we can overcome this crisis.

I want to believe that not only can we learn from this time, but we'll also emerge stronger. In each other's eyes, I see that the love that once connected us is still there - perhaps even in a new light.

It's in these small, yet meaningful moments when we're simply together and share with each other. And I've learned that it's important to consciously make time for one another.

<u>Essential:</u>

So, find intentional moments in your everyday life where you are there for each other without distractions. This shared time can help re-establish a deeper connection. Another important aspect is to maintain open and honest communication. Take the time to talk about your feelings without fear of hurt or misunderstanding. It's crucial to listen to each other and take each other's thoughts and worries seriously. This kind of exchange can help clear up misunderstandings and strengthen trust between you.

Today is our little daughter's birthday, and we have some guests over, which makes the situation between Roli and me quite challenging. I am still struggling with my emotions, which can erupt over everything and nothing at all right now. But today, I have to pull myself together because it's not about me. The guests should enjoy the celebration and not notice any of this. As best we can, we try to put on a good face for the ugly game. Or as I call it: charades, to convince our friends and family that everything is just fine with us.

Many people will know this game very well and have mastered the art of maintaining appearances perfectly. We, on the other hand, are failing miserably at it. Every time we touch, the tension in the air becomes palpable. More precisely, I tense up, while Roli tries to convince me with his affection that he loves me. But instead of easing the tension, it becomes more tangible with every touch.

When the first guests start to leave and a certain calm descends, Roli's sister approaches me. She has seen my posts on TikTok and asks directly what's going on. "Is everything okay with you guys?" Her eyes scan me with concern, and I realize that I can't avoid this any longer. So, I vaguely tell her what happened. With every sentence I reveal, her eyes widen. Confusion and disappointment flicker across her face. She is surprised by her brother's behavior, but also worried that this situation could destroy our relationship. "I need to smoke a cigarette first," she finally says. So we go outside to join the others. Since the kids are playing inside,

we can openly discuss the incident. It quickly becomes clear that both of his sisters are completely on my side. Only our daughter's godfather sees things a bit differently.
Not that he wants to downplay the incident, but he reasons: "Nothing really happened; it was just a few phone calls and a video that you both say isn't even worth watching. So why not let it go and trust that he'll never do something like this again?"

I feel my anger boiling over, and I respond in an agitated voice, "I should just let it go and trust?" I can't even finish my sentence before Roli's youngest sister interrupts me: "It's true that she needs to rebuild trust if she wants to save this relationship, but that takes time. Clearly, he made a huge mistake that none of us expected from him. But that shows how much you can be deceived by someone—no matter how long you think you've known them."

She pauses briefly, and you can see the disappointment and shock flash in her eyes as she glances briefly at her brother. Roli doesn't notice, as he is staring at the ground, looking dejected. One must give him credit: he could simply retreat inside and avoid the situation, but instead, he faces the questions and criticism like a man. He speaks without much thought, openly and honestly, even though he is visibly depressed. This is how we know and appreciate him, but today, it seems this side of him hardly touches anyone. The tension in the air is palpable, and while it hurts my heart to see him like this, my anger is simultaneously bubbling inside me. With every word that follows about this matter, it rises again.

The sister speaks again, this time more directly to me: "I'm a hundred percent behind you. If you say you want to get in the car and go to that woman, then we'll take my car and deal with it." Immediately, the second sister jumps in: "I'll pay for the gas and make sure you get the first punch in!" This unexpected turn elicits loud laughter from the group, breaking the tense atmosphere. It feels so good that I almost forget what we were just talking about. Roli looks up, grinning, and says, "I definitely don't want to miss that. What do you think, are you coming too?" he asks his only ally, the godfather. He nods and adds with a laugh, "I'll film the whole thing and put it online—as a cautionary tale of what happens when women go after each other."

The thought of breaking this "laughing hyena's" nose is tempting, but I know that reality looks different. Eventually, we wrap up the topic and head back inside. Only Roli stays outside, silently and pensively. He needs a few more minutes to himself before joining us.
After all the guests have left, I stand in the kitchen trying to tidy up. Wordlessly, Roli joins me, grabs a cloth, and begins drying the dishes. I ponder for a long time about what to say. Should I bring up the conversation we had outside, or should I make a joke and suggest that he fills up the car? After all, we have "a long drive ahead of us." But, as often happens, he beats me to it.

Gently, he wraps his arms around my waist from behind and pulls me closer. I feel his breath on my neck, and as I wring out the cloth, he presses closer to me. Just before I can tell him that I want to dry my hands quickly, he speaks up: "I'm

such an idiot. I almost destroyed everything I love with my blindness and stupidity."
His warm breath brushes against my skin, and instantly all my hairs stand on end. At that moment, I don't even know if I'm angry, sad, or turned on. Any other woman would probably have hit him with a frying pan, but I… I just can't help it. Slowly, I turn in his arms, look deep into his eyes, and see how deeply he is struggling. And that's what softens me—this look. Sincere, honest, full of remorse and pain. I believe him when he says he regrets it. And yes, I know that nothing happened. But it still hurts like hell! "I know I made a mistake," he says softly, his voice nearly breaking. "I never intended to hurt you."

I can hear the sincerity in his words, but at the same time, fear washes over me that we may not be able to return from this point. In that moment, I realize that it's not just about forgetting - it's about forgiving. To heal this pain, we both need to speak openly about our feelings, even if it's uncomfortable. I force myself to admit my fears and insecurities to him.

"I sometimes feel insecure when I see other women talking to you. It scares me that I'm not enough." It's a step I need to take to break down the wall between us.
His expression shifts from pain to understanding. "You are more than enough for me. I only want you," he says, pulling me closer.
In that moment, I feel that we are at a turning point. Perhaps we can not only survive this crisis but emerge from it stronger. I rest my head on his shoulder and take a deep

breath. It's not going to be easy, but I'm ready to work on us. Together.

<u>Listening and Understanding are Essential for a Strong Relationship</u>

Sometimes it's not just about what is being said, but also about how you listen. Take the time to truly understand the other person's perspective and show empathy. Asking questions and actively listening can help avoid misunderstandings and build a deeper connection. Working together to solve problems can strengthen your bond.

Making Time for Each Other:

Find intentional moments in your daily life where you can be there for each other without distractions. This shared time can help restore a deeper connection.

Open and Honest Communication:

You need to talk about what's on your minds without fear of hurt or misunderstandings. It's important to listen to each other and take each other's thoughts and concerns seriously. This kind of exchange can help clear up misunderstandings and strengthen the trust between you.
Reflection

To reflect on your relationship and work on the challenges that burden you, you need to take the time. Nothing can or will heal overnight. It requires **teamwork.**

Recognize that you must work on the relationship together. The challenges can make you stronger as a team. Become aware of how much you love each other and show each other your **appreciation** and affection.
Small gestures of love can make a big difference and strengthen your connection. Remember how it felt when you first fell in love - think back to the feelings you had during your first dates.

July 31. The Birth of the "Word Magnet" Account

We are on a road trip, and while we talk about everything under the sun, the conversation suddenly turns to my TikTok account. Roli looks at me and says, "You're always writing quotes about all kinds of topics. Sometimes they're funny, sarcastic comments, and other times they're profound thoughts about life or excerpts from your books." I nod, confirming his observation, and I'm curious where he's going with this.

"What do you think about creating a second account? A sort of group where you encourage others to post their own or their favorite quotes?"

The idea catches my attention. The thought of creating a space where not just I, but also other people can share their thoughts, wisdom, and perhaps even their worries, excites me. A place that thrives on many different voices rather than just my own.

But too soon I'm excited because anxiety sets in immediately. I have no idea how much work running a group involves, what I need to do, and how to "manage" the members. In short, I have no plan for anything like this. "I think your idea is great, but…" I pause to sort my thoughts, but Roli is already asking, "But?"

Resigned, I look at him and say, "I don't know how to get members, let alone what to do with all those people—if anyone is even interested in a group like this. Just thinking about having to create a WhatsApp group with all these separate sections like: chat, info, blah blah blah… I have no idea what else. I'm already hyperventilating." I symbolically grab my shirt and tug at it.

Gently, Roli places his hand on my lap and says, "Oh sweetheart, you're not alone. I'll help you. I'll set everything up on your phone, create the account, and give you tips on how to attract members. And of course, I'll promote your channel in my groups and on TikTok."

My heart leaps for joy, and for a brief moment, I fear I might have a stroke. My thoughts race, and a thousand ideas swirl through my mind.

When we get home, I immediately start working. For a moment, I push aside the gnawing fear that has been with me since Roli's suggestion. It's not just the uncertainty about what lies ahead - after all, I've never led a group on TikTok. From Roli's stories, I also know that there are often disputes among group members.

The thought that I might have to moderate and, in the worst case, mediate conflicts makes me nervous. Additionally, there's the immense work that falls to the founder, especially at the beginning. Building everything from scratch, organizing it, and keeping it active sounds overwhelming. But for now, I push that aside, and so a seemingly endless list of tasks to do emerges - which, of course, I want to go through with Roli. Excitedly, I rattle off point after point, and together we refine a plan on how to implement everything.

Within a few hours, the group is live on TikTok, the chat is
set up on my phone, and the first quotes are already saved as
drafts.
This again shows that Roli is simply the Steve Jobs 2.0 of the
situation: everything on my MacBook is perfectly prepared -
folders, lists, pictures - all the materials I need for my group
are ready.

In the first two days, I work like a madwoman on my quotes
and sayings. The promotional videos are already rolling, and
the views are impressive. The followers are still a bit
hesitant, but I'm optimistic that will change soon.
And it actually does. As soon as the TikTok account is set
up, a surprise comes just a few days later. Unbeknownst to
me, I sit at my computer when Roli sits down next to me
with his typical "I-have-something-for-you" face. Without
stopping my typing, I glance over at him with a smile and
wait eagerly for his big announcement.

His grin suggests that he has good news, which makes my
curiosity grow by the second. "Yes?" I ask exaggeratedly
kindly.
"Yes, you… listen," he begins.
"Yes?" I ask again.
"I have your first member for your group, if you want."
Immediately, I stop typing and stare at him wide-eyed.
"Really? Who?"
Again, he grins at me. "Someone from my TikTok group."
In my head, it immediately starts working. I go through all
the faces I know from his group. Great, that could be pretty
much anyone.
"Come on, tell me! Who?" I ask curiously.

"Angel."
With wide eyes, I look at him. "Oh, what? You have that duo thing going on with her, right?"
"Yes, exactly."
So Roli sends her a message to see if I can have her number so I can add her to the group. And just like that, she becomes my first member. Full of joy, we start filling the channel with quotes until, a few days later, the second member joins our group.
Simone, whom I shortly thereafter appoint as my admin. With each day that I spend at the computer or on my phone putting together images and quotes for my account, I notice how my writer's block slowly begins to dissolve.
Writing starts to bring me joy again, and the group is going really well. Although the group is growing slowly, the numbers are steadily rising, and I'm even making progress on my novel again. But that joy doesn't last long.
A few days later, I receive a voice message from Angel on WhatsApp: "Hi love, I wanted to ask if it's okay for you if I set up a separate chat to discuss more private matters."
Surprised, I agree and write Roli a message: "Hey babe, have you heard from Angel?"
No sooner has he read my message than he calls me. We talk briefly about it, and during that time, Angel sets up the new group chat.
She, Roli, my admin, and I are added. She gets straight to the point, and after a brief greeting, she uploads a few videos.
What I see then makes the old anger boil up inside me.
There's that face again - this woman, who depressively showcases her songs, mourning an unrequited love and the insurmountable disappointment. I can hardly believe it.
Does she never stop?

Does she really think this behavior will make Roli contact her? Or that any man would be impressed by this exaggerated show? This behavior is completely incomprehensible to me.

We begin sending voice messages back and forth, and in the meantime, I immediately block all her TikTok accounts. I also preemptively block her "friends." The others follow my example, and we agree to completely ignore her. So I try to redirect my attention back to my work and the group. But every day, something new comes up. Another video here, a message there - she is present everywhere again.
The discussions with Roli reignite, and unrest returns as if it were an unwelcome guest that has taken a permanent place at my table. As if that weren't enough, she also sends Roli a text message: "Emergency surgery tomorrow."
What the hell?! What's this nonsense now? I immediately confront Roli about it.
"What's that supposed to mean? Why didn't you tell me she texted you?"
He doesn't get a chance to respond because I bombard him with a flood of questions and old accusations. Of course, this doesn't help the situation, but my temperament gets the best of me once again.
Roli looks at me calmly, his voice steady as he says, "Sweetheart, I didn't tell you because I just skimmed the message and didn't pay attention to who it was from."
Instantly, doubt stirs within me as to whether this is really the truth, and my anger flares up again.
This time, however, before I completely lose it, he gently wraps his hands around my arms, looks me directly in the eyes, and repeats earnestly: "Sweetheart, I really didn't

realize it was her. If I had noticed, I would have told you right away. Or do you really think that if I wanted to hide it, I wouldn't just have deleted the message? After all the crap we've been through recently, and what you have to endure because of me, just because I'm an idiot who didn't notice what she's really up to?"

His eyes become moist, filling with tears, and the first one rolls down his cheek. "I love you. I don't want to lose you, and I definitely don't want you to feel bad because of me anymore."
His voice breaks on the last word, and I can no longer hold back either - the tears start flowing. Crying, we embrace, both unable to calm down. He repeatedly says, "I love you," and I respond, "I love you too." After what feels like an eternity of reassuring each other about how much we mean to one another, I finally let him go. We wipe the tears from our faces and sit down at the table. With a coffee for him and a glass of water for me, we slowly begin to calm down again.

Fearing that my writer's block might have crept back in, I sit down at the PC and start writing immediately. To my surprise, the words flow effortlessly; the chapters fill up, and the book continues to grow. This guide is fueled by the very emotions I'm trying to convey here. Whether I succeed fully remains to be seen. But right now, in this moment, I just want to write.

My therapy is writing. And I hope to reach as many people as possible with my experience to show them: "Hey, you're not alone." Roli and I have been a couple for 14 years, and

during that time, we've gone through so much - both good
and bad. And yet, we are still together.
"Love," you say? I say: not just love, but also understanding,
communication, and yes, even tears have accompanied our
relationship. The positive side of these turbulent years: our
bond has grown stronger with every hurdle we've overcome.
The discussions we've had have shown how much we care
for each other.
And the best part: my vocal cords are thicker than an opera
singer's - I can assure you of that!

Why is it so important to communicate with each other?

In difficult moments, especially during emotional conflicts
or misunderstandings, it is crucial to honestly and openly
share what you are feeling. How else is your partner
supposed to know what is weighing on you?
Often, such conflicts arise precisely because we don't
address misunderstandings or fears.
Don't hesitate to talk about your doubts or anxieties, as
otherwise, they can develop into bigger problems that are
even harder to solve.
A calm, open conversation can often help alleviate these
tensions.

Patience and Understanding

Try – even when it's damn difficult – to give your partner
space to explain their perspective during heated moments.
Controlling your emotions – yes, that would require a
separate guide – is not easy.

You'd prefer to make your point clear while armed with a frying pan, but you know that won't help. So, put the frying pan down, take a deep breath, and try to approach your partner with empathy. And no, *empathy* is not a new brand of cast iron pans. Empathy is that thing, that feeling you activate to perhaps understand the other person a little better.

Allowing Emotions

Sometimes tears and a good, honest cry help to release steam. After all, it shows that both are deeply affected and want to work on the relationship.
And let's be honest: Sometimes a little emotional outburst brings much more than all the silent moments of reflection combined.

Collaboration

Problems and challenges in a relationship are a shared matter. Instead of seeing them as separating factors, take the opportunity to find solutions together and emerge stronger as a couple.

<u>How does it continue?</u>

Well, after some time has passed, I can almost say that we have managed to master the situation. It's not perfect yet, but we are getting closer to our goal every day.
We talk much more about important things like "How are you today?" or "Can you tell me what happened today?"
These questions lead to topics that concern both of us and bring us closer together.

Our intimacy has also changed. He hugs me much more often and whispers to me, "I love you, my darling," or "I missed you today."
These little gestures are incredibly valuable to me and give me the feeling that we are close to each other again.
Our love life has also transformed. We are much more present with each other, looking into each other's eyes, holding each other, and kissing more intensely.
The frequency has massively increased.

I know it might seem like we found our way back to each other just because of this, but that's not the case. We had an active and fulfilling love life even before this situation. But now it feels more intense and real—I can't describe it any other way.
What I can say for sure is that I love him more than anything and I am so grateful that we faced this challenge together. Everything we have gone through has only brought us closer together—and I am sure that our relationship can gain even more depth now.

What I can also share with you:

Spend quality time together to strengthen your connection and leave everyday life behind. These evenings can help revive the romance.

Set Shared Goals:

By regularly taking the time to discuss your dreams and wishes, you can focus on the future and promote positive changes in your relationship. These shared goals not only strengthen your connection but also help deepen the trust and support you have for one another.

Finding Your Own Path:

There are times in life when we face difficult decisions. We cannot always foresee how things will develop, and sometimes it is unavoidable that relationships come apart. However, it is important to remain true to yourself and not lose sight of your own values and goals. Every step we take should bring us closer to the person we want to be.
Even though change can be frightening, it also offers the chance to begin something new and grow personally.

Reflect Together on Your Relationship:

Take the time to talk about the challenges and lessons you have experienced together. This can help strengthen your bond.

<u>**Recognizing Your Own Fears:**</u>

Take some time to think about your own fears and insecurities. Questions you might ask yourself include:
- What exactly makes me jealous?
- What past experiences might influence these feelings?
- Is there a behavior of another person that I absolutely cannot stand?

P.S.: I can only advise against pursuing a plan to remove someone who has hurt or harmed you from your life. Allow these people to continue to be part of your life, because nothing makes them angrier than seeing you happy. ;-)

<u>And the most important question of all:</u>

Do I feel comfortable and secure in the relationship?

A relationship should give you a sense of security, love, understanding, and just the right amount of craziness. It's a connection in which you feel safe and accepted while also being free to be yourself.

Avoid unhealthy comparisons

Focus on celebrating your own progress rather than comparing yourself to others—or worse, measuring your partner against others. After all, you got to know him just the way he is, with all his flaws and quirks. So don't even try to compare or change him.

In Italy, we have a saying for this:

Il lupo perde il pelo, ma mai il vizio

The wolf sheds its fur, but never its habits.

So don't even try to change him - you will fail miserably.

Set Personal Boundaries

Be aware of your personal values and boundaries. What is acceptable to you in a relationship, and what is not? Clearly defining your own boundaries can help you feel more secure and reduce jealousy.

Consider Professional Support

If jealousy is a constant issue in your life or relationship, it can be helpful to seek professional support. A therapist or counselor can help you explore the deeper causes of your jealousy and develop strategies to manage these feelings.

<u>Now Comes My Personal Conclusion</u>

Jealousy can be truly painful, but it also offers an opportunity for personal growth. When you take the time to reflect on yourself, strengthen your self-esteem, and set healthy boundaries, you can not only better manage your jealousy but also build a deeper and more harmonious relationship with yourself and your partner.

It's important to recognize and accept your own insecurities rather than ignore them. By being honest with yourself and understanding the reasons behind your jealousy, you can learn to let it go.
This takes time, but step by step, you can build trust - in yourself and in your partner. For me, this is still a significant challenge, but the more I write this guide, the more it helps me process everything.

Maybe writing is my secret remedy against jealousy! Jealousy can reveal what you need to work on. If you embark on this journey, you will notice how much inner peace and stability you can gain. In the end, it's about fostering a relationship based on trust and respect, rather than fear and control.

The Trigger of a Digital Escalation

It's just after 10:00 PM when a message from a friend in my group comes in: "The video I uploaded isn't directed at you."
Immediately, I'm curious. Roli is sitting next to me, and I ask him, "Did you read the message in the group chat?"
"In which chat?" he asks.
"Well, in the chat called 'Chit-Chat.'"
Shortly thereafter, the next message appears: "I'm being publicly shamed here."
With a pounding heart, I click on the link she sent, and immediately I notice her profile in the video. Someone is saying some nonsense about her while her TikTok profile is displayed.
"What the hell is this?" I ask Roli, who is just as stunned, staring at his phone, trying to make sense of it all.
From that evening on, everything takes its course—I simply have to react to this video.

The next day, I post my comment, but Roli is quicker and leaves his own, which triggers an avalanche of reactions. It starts subtly: at first, only isolated comments are made, then the attacks become harsher. Soon, it's not just us but also other members of our group who find themselves in the crosshairs. They are outright threatened.

The atmosphere becomes increasingly toxic, and out of fear of these cowardly attacks, some decide to leave the group. I can't just stand by and let this happen. So, I upload a video aimed at raising awareness about bullying. Roli speaks on his account as "Brother Roli" in his "Word for Sunday," also

discussing bullying. However, this video is taken by some as an opportunity to intensify their attacks on our group. The group of attackers deliberately investigates the accounts of our members. Since I was also active in the group and the related chat at that time, I was forced to take a stand. Ultimately, this led to a loud explosion. What angers me the most is the audacity of the lies being spread. It's hard for me to bear that they're trying to put me in my place. But when they attack my husband, that's where I draw the line.
I don't tolerate that and fight back loudly. And if my friend gets targeted too, then they've messed with the wrong person - three days later, I left the group.

The situation has calmed down somewhat since then, but it's far from over. However, we all stand by each other, especially behind her, and we will do everything we can to put an end to this nightmare.

Bullying is not an opinion – it is violence!

Whether online or offline: No one deserves to be humiliated, excluded, or threatened. We must not turn a blind eye when injustice occurs.

It is up to us to take responsibility and stand firm. Bullying is unacceptable in any form.
It must stop. Never forget:

Bullying is not a game!

Whether online or in real life, bullying leaves deep psychological and emotional scars. Any form of insult,

threat, or public humiliation can have serious consequences. If you are affected yourself or see someone being bullied, do not stay silent.
Talk about it, seek support, and take a stand against this form of violence.

My lesson from this?

Bullying can happen to anyone. I've realized how important it is to be brave and to stand up for others - even when it's uncomfortable. Stopping bullying is in our hands.

Bullying begins where empathy ends—we all have a responsibility to actively stand against it.

My personal story, along with my friend's, shows just how deeply the digital world can penetrate our real lives and cause immense harm. But it's not the technology itself that's the issue; it's the people hiding behind fake profiles, deliberately making life difficult for others. Whether out of boredom or a twisted sense of "fun," we are all responsible for our actions online.

That's why the rule is simple:

When your phone is on, your common sense should be on, too. Take a moment to consider the impact your words or actions might have on others before you post anything.

There's one more thing I absolutely need to get off my chest.

First:

If you feel that something is off in your relationship, or you suspect you're being misled, you're usually right. Trust your gut; it rarely deceives you. Follow up on it—take it from me, an everyday Sherlock who knows exactly what I'm talking about.

Second:

I have a deep-seated resentment toward these (anti)social media platforms. Even though I use them myself for certain purposes or as a distraction, I always draw a firm line: respect for others comes first, and I consciously distinguish between right and wrong.

The longer I spend on these platforms, the clearer it becomes how much people lose themselves in the digital world. A demeaning comment here, a nasty emoji there— and an innocent life can be deeply affected. It's terrifying to see just how out of hand things can get.

Never lose **respect** for others. Don't set your decency aside. But above all - and this is what matters most - pause for a moment before you comment, post, or message someone.

Ask yourself: how would the other person feel if I were to write something hurtful? Is it really worth it?

Imagine you're in a relationship: how would your partner feel if you were secretly messaging someone else?
You might think, "It's not physical, so it doesn't count as cheating if I'm just messaging someone."

Oh, really?

If it's truly harmless, then why not tell your partner? Why not mention that you're sharing intimate moments with this person, video chatting, or even exchanging pictures?
And now: does it still feel okay?

For me, anything that's done in secret crosses a line. If my partner feels uncomfortable doing something openly in my presence, then I have to ask: why do it in secret? Because they know it would bother me.

What they might not realize is how much angrier I'll be if I find out on my own. If they had taken a moment to consider whether it was truly right to be messaging others and exchanging pictures, they might have avoided a lot of pain.

Social media nearly destroyed our relationship – but through love and open communication, we've come out stronger.

In a world where distractions and challenges constantly bombard us, it's easy to lose sight of what truly matters. Ultimately, it all comes down to how we treat each other – both in the digital world and in real life. **Respect, honesty,** and **empathy** – yes, that strange yet powerful feeling, empathy – should be the foundation of every interaction. Each of us is responsible for our words and actions.

By being aware of the impact of our communication, we can not only avoid conflicts but also strengthen our relationships. Let's take a moment to pause and reflect before we act. In a fast-paced, often thoughtless world, small moments of reflection can bring about big changes. Every one of us has the power to make a positive difference – for ourselves and for those around us.

In our case, TikTok almost tore our relationship apart, and I'll admit, I played my part in letting it get that far. It's dangerous to take your partner for granted – a painful lesson I had to learn. But from this experience, Roli and I have learned to appreciate each other and make a conscious effort to spend quality time together.

<u>**Here are a few reflections that have helped me and might also inspire you:**</u>

What are my biggest insecurities in the relationship?

What positive qualities do I bring to the relationship?

How can I handle jealousy better in the future?

Take some time to reflect on these questions. They might help you gain clarity and move forward on your path.

Practical Exercises:

- Keep a journal where you write down your thoughts and feelings whenever you experience jealousy.
- Set small, achievable goals to boost your self-esteem, such as giving yourself one compliment each day.

Listen In!

I'd love to continue supporting you on your journey! In my podcast, *Liebeskiste*, I talk weekly with my husband about the everyday challenges in a relationship—and also about various other topics. You might find just the episode that inspires or helps you!

Important Takeaways

"Nothing is perfect, and it doesn't have to be. You can change your perspective and attitude to suit your needs. A relationship doesn't need to be perfect - it just needs to be real and work for both of you."

"Love is one of the strongest building blocks of any relationship, but the love you have for yourself is the foundation upon which it truly grows."

"If you don't want your phone to replace your partner, it's time to listen properly again. Put aside the flat device with the cold surface and give your partner your full attention."

Gwendoline P Point

Current Status

A few months after the difficult times in my relationship that taught me so much, I find myself sitting on the couch one evening again. I think about all the challenges we've faced together and feel how much our connection has changed.

We have talked a lot and opened up about our feelings, and I can see that we are on a better path. Despite the setbacks, I feel that we have both grown. That evening, I decide to take a step further. I pick up my phone and call Roli.

Instead of discussing problems or misunderstandings, I want to simply enjoy the moment and tell him how important he has become to me. "You know," I begin, "I am so grateful for everything we have been through. It has brought us closer, and I truly appreciate your strengths and the way you treat me."

He responds with surprise, but then he shares similar feelings. We begin to celebrate our love without the pressure of perfection. Instead of focusing on the negatives, we recognize how important it is to cherish the small things - the laughter we share, the support in tough times, and the closeness we have developed despite all the difficulties.

This simple conversation becomes a turning point for us. It reminds me that love doesn't have to be perfect; it just needs to be genuine and require the willingness to be there for each other during hard times. I learn that the decision to give and receive love not only strengthens our relationship but also helps me grow as an individual.

In that moment, I realize that we are not only talking about the challenges we've faced but also about the hope that now guides us. And so I conclude with the thought

that true love can flourish in its imperfection, as long as we are willing to embrace it.

"I sincerely wish you all the best on your
journey and hope that my experiences can help
you make the right decisions for yourself.
Remember, you are not alone—I understand
how you feel, and I am thinking of you."

Yours, Gwendoline

The Influence of Social Media on Relationships

In today's world, social media is an essential part of our lives. Platforms like Facebook, Instagram, and TikTok offer countless opportunities for interaction, communication, and networking. However, what seems so enticing in the digital realm can lead to problems in real life.

Social media has fundamentally changed the way we interact with one another. While it makes communication easier, it can also give rise to misunderstandings, jealousy, and trust issues. A study by ElitePartner shows that about 63% of respondents perceive social media as a stress factor in their relationship. The constant comparison with other couples often leads to dissatisfaction and can strain trust in one's own relationship.

Privacy and Digital Boundaries

Often, it is difficult to draw the line between private and public. Another problem is the sharing of images and videos that depict intimate moments. Such content is often disseminated without consent, which can trigger feelings of violation and distrust.
Researchers have found that younger people, in particular, are more susceptible to digital jealousy, which can negatively impact relationship dynamics.

My Recommendation:

Set clear boundaries for social media use in your relationship. Discuss what is acceptable for both of you and what is not.

- Talk openly about your online activities. Clarify misunderstandings before they escalate into problems—communication is key to building trust.

Diminished Intimacy

Social media can also lead to couples becoming less intimate with one another. Instead of having personal conversations, many people spend more time scrolling through their feeds or communicating online. This digital distraction can emotionally distance partners from each other and ultimately lead to estrangement. Constantly being immersed in the digital world can cause valuable moments in real life to be missed.

Studies show that couples who spend less time on their phones and actively engage in their relationship have a stronger emotional bond and are more satisfied.

What You Can Do:

- Schedule regular offline times when you can focus solely on each other—consider a weekly date night or a dinner together without digital distractions.
- Reduce social media usage during your time together. Put your phones aside to strengthen intimacy.

I wish you all the best, and if you'd like to read more, here's a list of my other books for you. (Currently, these books are only available in German):

Liebe in der Ehe
So entfachst du, das Feuer der Leidenschaft wieder neu.
Ratgeber
ISBN-13: 9783754347072

Das wahre Gesicht des Fetischs
Ratgeber
ISBN-13: 9783754373705

Seelenverwandtschaft entdecken
Das intime Beziehungsspiel mit 180 Fragen
in drei Kategorien
SBN-13: 9783756812387

So erziehst auch du k(l)eine Arschlöcher heran
Ratgeber
ISBN-13: 9783756211371

Zwischen Verlangen und Liebe
Roman
ISBN-13: 9783754355589